I have Someone to tell you

Confronting fear, shame, doubt, anger,
sadness, & pain with prayer

Lord, God, your light which dims the stars
Awakes all things,
And all that springs to life in you
Your glory sings.

Your peaceful presence, giving strength,
Is everywhere,
And fallen men may rise again
On wings of prayer.

You are the God whose mercy rests
On all you made;
You gave us Christ, whose love through death
Our Ransom paid.

We praise you, Father, with your Son
And Spirit blest,
In whom creation lives and moves,
And finds its rests.
Amen.

A suggestion on how to use this manual of prayer.

Take each section and spend at least 15-30 minutes meditating with it. Imagine each emotion in your heart. Feel the fear, shame, doubt, sadness, or pain and sense where you feel it in your body, mind, & soul. Allow yourself to be open to experiencing the emotion as it is.

Then Imagine Jesus present. Allow your heart to experience him near you, in your heart. See him transform each emotion into freedom and love.

At the end of each meditation, focus on the the phrase "who am I without this emotion." Let Jesus show you who you really are and spend a few moments thanking and praising Him.

∞∞∞∞

BEGINNING

Find a quiet place.

Breathe slowly and methodically.

Allow yourself to let go of your surroundings.

Feel your body.

What do you feel and where?

Feel your Heart.

What is weighing you down?

What is blocking you?

Feel your soul.

What do feel there?

Offer it all to the Lord.

Become

Aware

of

God's

presence

connecting

to

your

presence

Say the following slowly:

Lord!
I know you are here!
I know you hear me
and see me!
I come before your presence
with reverence!
I ask for the grace
to make this time
of prayer
fruitful!

"He said to them,

'Come, and you will see.'

So they went

and saw where

he was staying,

and they stayed with him

that day."

John 1:39 (NAB)

I have Someone to tell you!

"And only where God is seen does life truly begin.
Only when we meet the living god in Christ do we
know what life is. We are not some casual and
meaningless product of evolution. Each of us is
the result of a thought of God. Each of us is
willed, each of us is loved, each of us is necessary. There is nothing more beautiful than to be
surprised by the Gospel, by the encounter with
Christ. There is nothing more beautiful than to
know Him and to speak to others of our friendship
with Him."

Pope Benedict XVI   Homily April 24, 2005

∞∞∞∞

I see you, Fear!

I see you creep into my mind as if it were your personal playground. I see you play hide and seek with my emotions and dreams. I see you cast shade on the future as you try to swallow the light in the shadows. I see you fear and how you twist the truths about me and life and bury them in lies.

I see how you try to replace my true identity with false perceptions of judgments from my family, friends, the world. I hear the whispers you project into my heart, "what will they say" and "what will they think" and "What if I fail" and "How will I succeed." I see how your chains seeks to paralyse and convince me that I am no longer free to follow my dreams, to live my purpose with passion.

I see you.

I see you fear but you are not the only one there.

I see another more powerful than you. I see someone who is always near. He tells me who I am without you, fear. He calls me brother and sister and friend. He tells me he will never let me go. He holds me close to his heart.

I give you, fear, to the Lord of light. I cast your shadows into the light of his embrace, the brightness of his love, the warmth that scatters the chills of doubt you bring.

I see you and I see Him. He is life. You are nothing. He is truth and you are not. He is warmth and freshness and hope. He is freedom to proceed. He is everything. He is the one who said have no fear I have already conquered the world.

I see you, Lord. I see your strength and security. I see You. In your name, Jesus, I open my heart and invite you to stay. In your name, Jesus, I purge the fear and I proclaim the truth in freedom you bring.

I see You, Lord! I feel you in my heart. You show me who I am without fear.

Jesus is truth. Jesus is life. Jesus is warmth. Jesus is hope. Jesus is freedom. Jesus is everything.

∞∞∞∞

I see you, shame!

I see how you squirm and slither through my consciousness. I feel you slimy and cold. I feel your uneasiness that hides in my unconscious places. I know you are there. I see the burden of guilt that has become the yolk I wear. I feel its weight upon my shoulders and the tension in my neck and head.

I see how you lead me to underestimate my value and worth. I see how you drive me to choose lesser things, to settle for less, to indulge my self in relationships with material things or people that leave me empty. I hear your voice in my heart cry out, "I am not good enough", "I will never measure up", "I don't deserve happiness", "I am unworthy of forgiveness", "I am unlovable."

I see you. I see you shame but you are not the only one there.

I see another more powerful than you. I see someone who is always near. He tells me who I am with out you, shame. He calls me lover. He shows me fullness and joy that last.

I see you, Lord. I give you this shame. I see how you reclaim my worth. I see in you, through you, my true self. I feel your presence around me. You have made my heart your dwelling. You have chosen me. You choose me a new each day. You transform the shame and guilt into mercy and love. I am forgiven. I am loved in you. You have made me lovable.

I see you, Lord. In your name, Jesus, I open my heart and I welcome my true identity and worth. I see you tell me who I am without shame.

∞∞∞∞

I see you, doubt!

I see you doubt and darkness. I feel your presence. I see how you cast shade upon hope's bright promise. I see your finger smudges on the worry and anxiety that enter my thoughts. I see you broadcast the confusion that weighs heavy upon my journey.

I see you cloak the present moment with your haze of uncertainty. I see the fog that hinders my next step in the present moment of life.

I see you. I see you doubt but you are not the only one there. I see another more powerful than you.

I see someone who is always near. I see someone who is light, in whom there is no darkness and for whom darkness is like the light of day. He tells me who I am with out you, doubt.

He cast uncertainty and confusion aside with His trust. He calls me loyal friend and companion. Though I am weak and frail and may falter, He will never deny me or waiver in his trust in me.

I see you, Lord. I give you this doubt. I see you are the refuge of my life, my strong shelter. I see you calm the storms. I see you hold me in the palm of your hand. I see your plan for me; I see the future of great expectation. I see you and I trust you. In trusting you, I trust me. I cast the doubt into the burning fire of your love that consumes the haze of uncertainty and breathes forth clarity.

I see you Lord and I praise you and thank you. I trust you in all things. I allow your power and the clarity of your name to echo forth in the depth of my being. I see you and I come to you.

In your name, Jesus, I purge this doubt into the bright clarity of your promise that you know my life as it unfolds. I see you, Lord. I see you show me who I am without this doubt.

∞∞∞∞

I see you, anger!

I see you anger. I see you deep within me. I see how you fume and fuss like an erupting volcano. I see how you work on my feelings of frustration and pain. I see how you drive me to point the finger of blame.

I see you smoulder and spark. I see you anger. I see how you direct me to accuse the other and never see the source within. I see you anger. I see you want me to blame and fight and kick with all my might. I see you guide me to be short tempered and easily annoyed. I see you want me to build walls to keep people out. I see you want me to hold on to grudge and revenge; I see how this only weighs me down. I see you want me to hold back forgiveness. I see you want me to make demands rather than seek to be reconciled. I see you.

I see you anger but you are not the only one there. I see another more powerful than you. I see someone who is always near. I see someone who brings peace where chaos rages. I see him touch the anger and it transforms into passion and love. He tells me I am not the anger. He tells me who I am with out you, anger. He calls me his peace. He calls me strength and love.

I see you, Lord. I see you and claim your promise that all things work for good for those that love you. I see you are the Lord not of blame but of solutions. I see you Lord. I see how all things are for your glory and that frustration and pain are pointers to deeper places of healing and wholeness you want for me. I see you lead me to a place of mercy, for-giveness, and acceptance of myself and others.

In your name, Jesus, I let the fire of anger be transformed by your unconditional pas-sion for me. I see you anger and I give you to the Lord in peaceful surrender. I see you Lord

and I thank you and praise you. I see you tell
me who I am without this anger.

∞∞∞∞

I see you, sadness!

I see you sadness and despair. I see how you try to ensnare the hope blossoming in my heart. I see how you blind me to the future filled with possibilities by the mask of yesterday's loss. I feel your uneasiness. I see you chase away laughter and joy. I see how you let guilt tell me I can no longer live and love. I see you trap my joy beneath a suffocating blanket of guilt about the past.

I see you sadness. I see how you attack me from within to imprison me. I see with you life loses its luster and spark. I see the gray haze by which you colour my experiences. I feel the disappointment and the misery you bolster in my heart. I see how you want me to hold on to the loss and not be consoled. I see how you whisper that "no one understands my loss", "that if I laugh and enjoy then I betray what or who I lost."

I see you, sadness. But I see you are not the only one there. I see another more powerful than you. I feel his presence in my heart.

I see someone who says sadness is found in happiness also. I see someone who is joy to the world even in suffering and loss. He tells me who I am with out you, sadness. He calls me the reason of his joy. He leads me to the brightness that he brings as I let him lead me forward. He shows me that to enjoy is to celebrate love shared and magnify the memories I hold on too.

I see you, Lord. I see you as the anchor of hope for all that I experience in life. I see you dance on the seas of life. I see you Jesus. I see you weep for your friend Lazarus and continue to love and laugh. I invite you into my life.

In your name, Jesus, I give you this grief and sadness that has penetrated my being. I see you, Lord. I see you tell me who I am without this sadness.

∞∞∞∞

I see you, pain!

I see you pain. I feel your presence. I see the tears that fall on the inside. I see the thoughts that no one cares and no one understands. I see the bruised and battered heart that longs for comfort and consolation.

I see you pain. I see how you camouflage and colour every experience in life. I see the hurt that invites me to close my heart to others. I see you and how you want me to compare myself to others. I hear the questions you pose in my heart "why now?" and "why this?" and "what did I do to deserve this?" I see how you want me to isolate myself from my friends, my family, from the world.

I see you. But I see you are not the only one there. I see another more powerful than you. I feel his presence. I see someone who has taken on my pain. I see someone who has claimed my pain for himself. I see him trans-form pain into a new way of openness.

I see you, Lord. I see you high on the cross. I see your pain. I place my pain in the palms of your hands. I see you reach and touch the deepest place of my woundedness. I feel your warmth. I feel your presence in my heart. I see you cry out to the Father and take all my cries with your cry to Him. I hear you say by your wounds I am healed and comfort-ed.

I see you in my pain and weakness and I feel your strength enter into me. I see you.

I see you, Lord. I see you call forth my true identity. I am yours and you are mine and

we journey together.   In your name, Jesus, I
let go of my pain and feel the presence of your
resurrected glory.   I see you tell me who I am
without this pain.

∞∞∞∞

I see Someone who is always near.   I feel his
presence in my heart, mind, and soul.   I see
nothing I do can change his love for me.

I see someone whose name brings strength and
peace; I see Someone who shows me who I am
without fear, shame, doubt, anger, sadness, &
pain.   I see someone who tells me who I am and
I am loved, I am necessary, I am wanted.   In
your name Jesus, I open my heart to you and I
let you enter. I see you tell me who I am!

∞∞∞∞

I have someone to tell you.
Come and see!

"He said to them,
"Come, and you will see."
So they went and saw
where he was staying,
and they stayed with him
that day."
John 1:39

∞∞∞∞

Lord, God, your light which dims the stars Awakes all
things,
And all that springs to life in you
Your glory sings.

Your peaceful presence, giving strength,
Is everywhere,
And fallen men may rise again
On wings of prayer...

∞∞∞∞

26

Thank you!
May the goodness of God
continue to lighten your journey.
May his closeness strengthen you!
May His healing bring you wholeness.
May His love be your love.
May His presence carry you
onward and upward.

67065289R00017

Made in the USA
Middletown, DE
19 March 2018